Crosswords for Seniors

Active Brain Edition Vol 5

SPEEDY
PUBLISHING

Puzzle #1
Follow the Conductor

Across

1. Fearsome snakes

7. (of words) formed in imitation of a natural sound

13. Depraved

14. Delicate lace

16. One on the way in

17. Mosaic piece

18. Shaver

19. Plan in advance

21. Nashville sch.

22. Burned up

24. Canary relative

25. Driving pegs

26. Play at a faster tempo, on sheet music: Abbr.

28. Shatner's sci-fi drug

29. Stress test measure

30. Delicious diet-breaker

33. Pucker producer

34. Payback factor

40. Belt inserts

41. 1992 Best Actor nominee

42. Browning title character

43. ___ account (never)

44. Dnieper tributary

46. Prejudice

47. Up

48. Country folk

50. Early iMac display

51. Reddish-brown horses

53. of or relating to the island or republic of Malta or its inhabitants

55. Subject to court proceedings

56. Some satellite launchers

57. ___ horoscope

58. E or G, e.g.

Down

1. Large butterfly

2. Like the Carbide and Carbon building

3. Field fare, for short

4. Sound from the belly of the beast?

5. Unoriginal actors

6. They're usually even on one side

7. Eschew table manners

8. Jones of the Miracle Mets

9. Archaic bidding

10. Appliance buttons

11. Summertime quenchers

12. Old tummy tuckers

13. belonging to or prescribed for celiac disease

15. Sartre novel, with "La"

20. Nicest looking

23. Actress Yvonne

25. One of 14, for humans

27. Place

29. Egyptian for "be at peace"

31. Fish story

32. Denver clock setting: Abbr

34. I'd like to propose ...

35. Wrench

36. With vigor

37. Lacking vigor

38. More thinly sown

39. Preferences

44. without liveliness

45. Without - in the world

48. Ms. McEntire

49. Squint-eyed opening

52. "Far out!"

54. Body art, briefly

Puzzle #2
Indian Spices

Across

1. Spice in curry

6. a risky and uncertain venture

15. What's in -?

16. "'Deed I Do" singer

17. Early part for Dustin

18. Not randomly arranged

19. Countertenor

20. Pith

21. Older couple's home, often

22. Box-score Indians

23. Cost

24. Magritte and Russo

25. Pellet shooter

27. Torment

28. Checks to make sure

29. Vane dir.

31. Renée of 'The Big Parade'

32. Commercial come-on

37. 'Exodus' character

39. Darling

40. Y2K Eminem song

43. Ones getting "worry lines"?

45. Feed -, starve...

46. Mother Teresa, notably

47. W.C. Fields persona

48. Rummy laydowns

49. Relatives of arians

50. Attention-getters

51. Some appetizers

53. Abba hit of 1976

54. Causes of many swoons

55. Palm leaf

56. Miscellanies

57. Year, to Yves

Down

1. any of various long-legged carrion-eating hawks of South America and Central America

2. Alone

3. Concern

4. Pointer Sisters' '__ Excited'

5. Classical introduction?

6. Customers

7. Nobelist Dulbecco

8. France in letters

9. Not, in Nantes

10. Cause of freezing, perhaps

11. Social stinger

12. Align, in a way

13. Quick round of tennis

14. Tries out

20. Expert

23. Shine partners?

26. Individually

30. Fixed gazes

33. Hall of Famer Tittle, for short

34. a mistake resulting from neglect

35. an alkaloid poison that occurs in tobacco

36. of the eastern part of a city e.g. Manhattan

38. Cutting tooth

39. Seaplane inventor Glenn

40. Part of an act

41. Pre-Aztec Mexican

42. Classic early press

44. Where the Latino Walk of Fame is

45. "___ should keep himself to himself": "Treasure Island"

50. Weaver's bobbin

52. Ending on lime

53. "__ tree falls ... "

Puzzle #3
Trip To-Do List

Across

1. Residents of dry, open country in South America

9. Nicholas Gage book

14. Wrap around

15. Dodges

16. He played Benjamin Franklin Pierce

17. Deadly

18. Old Glory designer

19. "Shoot!"

21. ___-relief

22. In a breezy manner

24. Dr. of hip-hop

25. determine or distinguish the nature of a problem or an illness through a diagnostic analysis

27. Letters on seconds

29. Start of an itinerary

30. Foul moods

31. Catalogs

34. Affixes, as a decal

36. ....good example

37. Bold poker words

39. Jog

40. Makes manifest

43. Stat for Schilling

44. Made out

45. Thimbleful

47. Romanov duchess

49. Basic French verb

50. relating to or near the female labium

51. Ring leaders?

54. Time wasters

55. devouring or craving food in great quantities

56. Down providers

57. Accents

Down

1. Transmission

2. Get rid of

3. 'Open' autobiographer

4. Ana

5. Altar constellation

6. Year Marcian became emperor

7. What the Constitution is called

8. Green-blue paint hue

9. First name in stunts

10. Follower of an extra-long workday

11. Portrayer of John McCain in 'Game Change'

12. Closer by

13. Archipelago makeup: Abbr.

15. ___ May Clampett of 'The Beverly Hillbillies'

20. *The die is cast

22. Where Plato shopped?

23. Arctic native

26. Reasons for excommunication

28. Nine-digit ID

30. 1960 Everlys hit

31. Halifax hrs.

32. Woo, in a way

33. Like many root vegetables for the winter

35. Vex a lot

38. Leaves the rat race

41. Cosmetician Lauder and others

42. Nadia Boulanger's "La ___ "

44. Tight group

46. Swattable sorts

47. Former HBO persona

48. Animal Collective singer Avey

49. Dwarf planet that dwarfs Pluto

52. PETA bête noire

53. Before, in verse

Puzzle #4
World Geography

Across

1. Editing "never minds"

6. Quickly repealed statute

14. Bring up the rear

15. Like blue-ribbon-winning steak

17. View anew

18. Some appetizers

19. Favoring common folk

21. Roll up

22. Loud speaker

23. Distress

25. Mediterranean isl.

26. Kind

28. Shoot over

29. Seven-time winner of the World Match Play Championship

30. Sartre novel, with "La"

32. Old atlas abbr.

33. Meandering

34. Peacock's nest?

37. Parrot

38. Sea soarer

41. Wipes out

43. Notes below las

45. Superman nemesis Luthor

46. Milk curdler

47. What some shots prevent

49. Antonym of exo-

50. Doesn't support a conspiracy theory?

52. How campers may sit

55. Cheech of comedy

56. a metric unit of length equal to ten meters

57. Father/son statesmen of England

58. Does some interior decorating

59. Oldtime daggers

Down

1. German thoroughfare

2. a drug (trade name Trental) used to treat claudication

3. Spring times

4. Relate

5. Falls icily

6. "For an avid philatelist like me, sorting envelopes is thrilling - I might spot a ___!"

7. Fair sight

8. Kitty contribution

9. Start of the 16th century

10. ___ squad

11. Former Palestinian leader

12. Pauses during speech: Var.

13. Features of some sandals

16. a device for emptying a cask by tilting it without disturbing the dregs

20. Most lamebrained

23. Bridge supports

24. Wide shoes

27. Western bulrushes

31. Abalone eaters

33. Answer to the riddle "Dressed in summer, naked in winter"

34. Moon of Neptune

35. Funnyman David

36. "Sex and the City" author Bushnell

38. Goal of some Río Bravo crossers

39. Bring together again

40. Resets

42. Moviegoer's chocolate bite

44. Philatelist's quest

48. Car racer Prost

50. Entr'___

51. Sharp

53. ___ little teapot ...

54. Agent

Puzzle #5
Beautiful Melodies

1	2	3		4	5	6	7	8			9	10	11	12
13			14						15		16			
17											18			
19									20					
21					22			23						
24				25						26				27
			28			29		30						
31	32	33	34				35							
36						37								
38						39					40	41	42	
	43			44		45				46				
47				48				49						
50				51										
52				53										
54					55						56			

Across

1. "Prince ___" ("Aladdin" song)

4. Hidden wealth

9. Con game

13. Like tiny tots

16. Emporio ___

17. Still developing

18. D-Day fleet

19. A thorough insurance adjuster ____

21. Classic cars

22. Sound from a flat

23. ___ Wrap

24. Familiar address

25. Paulo preceder

26. Go up against

28. Off-white hue

30. Take ___ of absence

31. Suppositions

36. Currencies

37. Dark times in verse

38. Having zero gravity

39. Some NFLers

40. Pot-pie veggie

43. Ring ___ (sound familiar)

45. ___-relief

46. Blunders at Fenway

47. Unrealistic hope

50. "... smile be your..."

51. Buoyancy

52. "Up and ___!"

53. Some successful runners

54. Pop

55. ___ de Torquemada (Spanish Inquisition leader)

56. Ogee shape

Down

1. Condense on a surface

2. Ach du ___!

3. 'We have so much in common!'

4. Truck-stop sight

5. Does, as business

6. Shows peevishness

7. Cutting remarks

8. Pacesetter

9. Managers work for them

10. Tapioca-yielding plants

11. Church foyer

12. Overlook

14. Perennial herb of East Indies to Polynesia and Australia; cultivated for its large edible root yielding Otaheite arrowroot starch

15. Shannon and others

20. lacking external ears

25. Congers

27. Guitar pro Paul

29. Quiet ending?

30. Marge's sister, to Bart Simpson

31. U.K. record label

32. Fund

33. continuing at full strength or intensity

34. Widescreen process

35. Parachuting florist's cry as he leaves the plane?

40. "The Scarlet Letter" woman

41. Builds

42. Eyeball

44. Italian river valley in W.W. II fighting

45. Hershey alternative

46. Wide shoe spec

47. Freddy Krueger and others

48. Abbreviation for non entity, a person bereft of personality and conversational skill.

49. Brothers and sisters

Puzzle #6
Friends with Benefits

Across

1. Laugh riot

7. a woman who is a man's sweetheart

15. Prefix with magnetic

16. not liable to error

17. What higher prices may produce

19. Nintendo's Super ___

20. Market surpluses

21. Job for Poirot

22. Major record label

23. Sartre novel, with "La"

24. Method: Abbr.

25. Readiness to produce meals for G.I.'s?

28. Some Tuscans

29. The "S" in R.S.V.P.

30. "___ bien!"

31. Bishop of Rome

34. Aurora's counterpart

36. Pooh-pooh

39. Polishing machines at an Ithaca campus?

43. Department store department

44. Adjusts, as tires

45. Abbr. in a resort's name

46. 180° from NNW

47. Certain print

48. Nearby

49. It often has islands

54. having or involving three colors

55. Full of complexities

56. lacking seeds

57. French president's residence

Down

1. John, Paul and George: Abbr.

2. Take the risk

3. One opening a jail door, say

4. "So ___ to you, Fuzzy-Wuzzy": Kipling

5. Mornings, for short

6. Certain riding horses

7. Neglect

8. Merger

9. French diplomat who supervised the construction of the Suez Canal (1805-1894)

10. Computer monitor, for short

11. Bank offering, for short

12. Kwan and Kerrigan

13. Protect, in a way

14. Boom source

18. Rinse, as with a solvent

22. A foot has 305 of these: Abbr.

23. "Rob Roy" star, 1995

24. Stored, as fodder

26. Bad looks

27. Changes color, maybe

32. Mixes before cooking

33. electro-acoustic transducer for converting electric signals into sounds

35. Mariner's measure

36. Noncommissioned officers ranking above corporal and below sergeant first class

37. Broadway character who sings "Tea for Two"

38. Dungeons & Dragons game co.

39. The Italian version of the given name Caesar

40. Infant bodysuit

41. South American plains

42. Water measurement

43. Ones graded E-8 in the Army

48. "That's not ___!" (parent's admonishment)

50. Cause of some repetitive behavior, in brief

51. Chat room abbr.

52. Sports org. with the Calder Cup

53. "The Steve Allen Show" regular

Puzzle #7
Word Play

Across

1. Williams title starter

7. Change channels?

13. Figures of speech?

15. Et ___

16. Be no slouch in class?

18. Magnetic induction units

19. "Welcome" site

20. Like fingerprints

22. "Fables in Slang" author

23. 50%

25. Used as a dining surface

26. French tire

27. Glacial ice formation

29. Brits' thank-yous

30. Go over

31. Nonreaders

34. Rum/vodka cocktail

35. a person who seizes or arrests (especially a person who seizes or arrests in the name of justice)

36. any of a number of tiny parallel grooves such as: the scratches left by a glacier on rocks or the streaks or ridges in muscle tissue

37. Charlotte-to-Raleigh dir.

38. any of various plants of the genus Sedum

42. River that's the site of Javert's demise in "Les Mis

43. Bank job

45. Boxer Oscar ___ Hoya

46. Hebrew letter

47. Eponymous rink jump

49. Atl. crosser

50. Concerned relatives group

52. Girl of old comics

54. Chopper parts

55. Bingeing

56. Upright, inscribed stone tablets

57. Discussion conclusion

Down

1. any of various mostly Mexican herbs of the genus Cosmos having radiate heads of variously colored flowers and pinnate leaves

2. French rocket

3. Rag

4. Native: Suffix

5. Neighbor of Swed.

6. 1986 self-titled album whose cover was Andy Warhol's last work

7. Classic McDonnell Douglas aircraft

8. Bassoon, e.g.

9. Aliens, for short

10. Manhattan street leading to the Williamsburg Bridge

11. Good eggs

12. Relax

14. Fish in a firth?

17. Flip side of Elvis's "Jailhouse Rock"

21. Become smitten with

24. Kind of curve

26. Diminished, with "out"

28. "The Nutcracker" lead

30. Casino gear

32. End of many an E-mail address

33. Circular: Abbr.

34. Low Army rank

35. Gorged oneself

36. Red giants with zirconium oxide in their spectra

39. Abandon

40. Heavy overcoat

41. tangled in a dense mass

43. Medieval merchants' guild

44. Add up

47. Short-billed rail

48. "There ___ young..." (common limerick start)

51. Cambodia's Lon ___

53. Some G.I. duties

Puzzle #8
Ask a Mathematician

Across

1. Interpreted to be

7. Guffaw components

10. Nutritional fig.

13. Writer St. John ___

14. Lookouts, sometimes

17. Atonement

18. Lethargic feelings

19. Patronize, as a restaurant

20. Hold-up man?

21. Marked down

22. Greenhouse gadgets

24. 9 + 3 + 1 + 1/3 + 1/9 + ..., e.g.

27. Have ___ of mystery

28. Wall St. type

29. Mideast plant favored by Scrabble players

32. Lucknow title

34. Videogame initials

35. U.S. codebreakers

36. Spat-following letters

37. German indefinite article

39. Elbert Hubbard work, with "A"

47. Squared masonry stones

48. Old music halls

49. Monster: Prefix

50. cause to be out of tune

51. Magnetic coil

54. One way to get wet

55. Acceptance as true

56. Deposed leaders, often

57. Pink Floyd's Barrett

58. MSN or AOL

59. 'Thy Neighbor's Wife' author

Down

1. Salty guy

2. Royal pelt

3. Still

4. Start of many a workday

5. 'Let's go!' to Nadal

6. Trio + trio

7. Prosciutto, e.g.

8. Lawyers' org.

9. Ethopian emperor Haile

10. Floral specialist

11. Valets, at times

12. Pompous sort

15. Shreds

16. Mosaic repairer

22. Calc. calculation

23. Defensive response to a doubter

25. Poet __ Maria Rilke

26. Fed. loan group

29. Iranian city, or its river

30. Involving luck

31. fringed or adorned with tassels

32. Shipping route

33. Ziti alternative

38. S.f. characters

40. Ripped-off item

41. Lancelot player in "Camelot"

42. an accessory or adjoining anatomical parts or appendages (especially of the embryo)

43. Full price

44. Join together

45. Belly button types

46. In ___ (sort of)

51. Symbols for scandium

52. Microchips (abbr.)

53. Sheriff's aide (abbr.)

Puzzle #9
Environmentally Aware

Across

1. Come into one's own

8. Ballet-company stars

15. a flowering shrub

16. Journalism legend Ida

17. Diplomatic achievement

19. Sea birds

20. Lapses into error

21. Irish Sea feeder

22. There's nothing　!

23. Not true, in a way

24. Parasite site

25. Bambi's aunt

26. Rockslide debris

27. W.C. Fields persona

28. Link

30. Sang loudly

31. Boldly patterned warblers

33. Archipelago components

36. Goes here and there

40. Extends across

41. Hits, runs, and errors

42. DDE opponent

43. Ganja

44. Sources of prized roe

45. Pound notes?

46. Pupil's place

47. Nightclub

48. Rosacea and others

49. "I must submit to an epitaph graven by a fool" penner

52. someone whose income is from property rents or bond interest and other investments

53. Cuts off

54. Ushers

55. Some religious fundamentalists

Down

1. Sans-serif typeface

2. Inside track

3. Facing a jury

4. Medical insert

5. Without

6. Que. neighbor

7. They know the score

8. Prima ballerina

9. Mastodon trap

10. Traffic regs., e.g.

11. There: Lat.

12. Direct to the exit

13. Italian sports apparel company

14. Was far from clement

18. Cuba, once, to the Soviet Union

23. Low-pH compounds

24. "The Planets" composer

26. Editing "never minds"

27. Small paving stones

29. Former Israeli minister Moshe

30. Other people's kids?

32. Learning environments

33. Ticket givers

34. McDonald's mascot before Ronald

35. Layered entree

37. Seriously sincere

38. Jump ball tosser

39. 1973 man-becomes-cobra movie

41. Flu symptom, with "the"

44. Cobbler, at times

45. When Othello arrives in Cyprus

47. Cracker spread

48. Fungal spore sacs

50. Worker doing a case study: Abbr

51. Chopping part of a chopper

Puzzle #10
The Greatest Fictional Love Stories for All Time

1	2	3	4	5	6	7		8	9	10	11	12	13	14
15								16						
17								18						
19							20							
21				22		23				24				
25			26		27			28	29					
30				31		32						33	34	35
36					37					38				
39				40					41					
			42					43		44				
45	46	47				48			49		50			
51				52	53			54		55				
56							57							
58							59							
60							61							

Across

1. Dress

8. The Southwest's ___ Desert

15. People holding signs at airports

16. Rival for Marius's love

17. Maintain, as attention

18. Entangled by

19. Characters in "Romola" and "The Gondoliers"

20. Coastal flier

21. Victorian, for one

22. Dry, in Durango

24. Unaccompanied part songs

25. a rapid series of short loud sounds (as might be heard with a stethoscope in some types of respiratory disorders)

27. Big eyes, metaphorically

30. Prepares to fire

32. Fairy tale figure

33. Simple fastener

36. Michael Crichton best seller, with "The"

39. Criminal patterns, for short

40. Earthy deposits

41. Peter, Paul or Mary

42. Certain services

44. Bygone blade

45. Outfit

48. Jet-setters' jets, once

50. an agency established in 2001 to safeguard United States transportation systems and insure safe air travel

51. lacking rain

54. a mattress filled with straw or a pad made of quilts

56. Opens

57. Actress once featured in ads for Chanel No. 5

58. haircut in which the head is shaved except for a band of hair down the middle of the scalp

59. Persian Gulf sight

60. Revolvers

61. Gives a number to

Down

1. an industrial center and the nominal capital of the Netherlands

2. The New Yorker contributor until 1968

3. Vegan side dishes

4. Peloponnesian War participant

5. ___ a beet

6. Gets the lead out?

7. "Saving Private Ryan" craft: Abbr.

8. Covered with many small figures, in heraldry

9. Suffix with my-

10. "I'd do it all over again"

11. Father-and-daughter actors

12. Chain of hills

13. of or like a feeble old woman

14. Bogotá babies

20. marked by absence of sound

23. They're not allowed to travel

26. Airport alternative to JFK or LGA

28. Ocean liners?

29. Dash lengths

31. Here or there

33. His self-titled book has 24 chapters

34. Score after a tie-breaking safety

35. Hill predators

37. Kid's cry

38. Dorm overseers, for short

42. Get a program on the radio

43. Tampa neighbor, informally

45. a bad-tempered person

46. What las novelas are written in

47. Campbell of "Martin"

49. Arabian capital

52. Israeli resort

53. I.R.S. ID's

55. Advance

57. the federal department responsible for safeguarding national security of the United States

Puzzle #11
Tools for Mass Production

Across

1. ___ Energy (big natural gas utility)

6. Cable inits.

9. "___ die for!"

14. ___-Meal (vacuum food storage system)

15. Followers of some asterisks

17. Municipal dept.

18. To the degree that

19. Suffix with exploit

20. Singer Lopez

21. "I" problem

22. Some tracks

24. Name dropper?

26. Environs

28. Positions

30. Certain supermarkets, for short

31. Come to pass

32. Job for a speech coach

36. Bar

37. Ravel's "___ Antique"

38. Gentle

39. Put on, as cargo

40. Avoids

45. Lives

47. Bowls

48. ___ anglais (English horn)

49. First six tracks, say

51. James Bond's "A View to ___"

52. Kind of surgery

54. McEntire and others

55. Stinging jellyfish

56. ___-Whirl

57. Chips in

58. Artist's asset

59. Olden daggers

Down

1. Lash out at

2. La Scala, e.g.

3. Crackpot

4. "Twelfth Night" countess

5. Signal receivers

6. Throw ___

7. 1820 White House residents

8. Richard Wagner's second wife

9. Intermittently

10. Shelley's "___ Skylark"

11. Provider of some outdoor entertainment

12. Shade lighter than palmetto

13. ___ buco

16. "Beloved" author Morrison

23. "Full House" star

25. Summit

27. Soldier

29. Simple fastener

31. Nathan and others

32. Letters of sizes

33. Rip into

34. Have too little

35. Mardi Gras, e.g.: Abbr.

36. Massenet's "Le ___"

38. Cheap

40. Calm

41. Earn

42. Like some mushrooms

43. "Ecce homo" speaker

44. Dances energetically

46. Losing proposition?

48. ___ Nostra

50. Suit to ___

53. 22.5 degrees

Puzzle #12
Weber's Best

Across

1. Biases

7. There may be money in it

14. "Forget about it!"

15. Like some oil

16. Mame, for one

17. Set sail

19. Really good one

21. Tarzan creator's monogram

22. "Good grief!"

23. Airs

24. Edison's middle name

25. "___ Freischütz" (Weber opera)

26. Era

27. Met expectations?

28. Funnel-shaped

29. Grosse ___, Mich.

30. Skinflint

33. Fast-food chain

34. Protesters' cries

35. ___-cochere (carriage entrance)

36. Celebrity photographer Herb

37. Arabian capital

38. The Braves, on scoreboards

41. ___ line (major axis of an elliptical orbit)

42. Angling equipment

43. City on the Yamuna River

44. File on an iPod

45. Check mate?

47. Big ray

49. Hyper, impatient ones

50. 1960 Bobby Rydell hit

51. Confine

52. Property recipient, at law

53. having or joined by a seam or seams

Down

1. Didn't go straight

2. a room (as in a hotel or airport) with seating where people can wait

3. Comparatively close

4. Eminent

5. Mai ___

6. Qaddafi has a slew of them

7. Like some muscles

8. Goes off

9. Fills

10. ___'acte

11. "Flying Down to ___"

12. Hospital supply

13. Weaken

18. Puts down

20. Anouk of "La Dolce Vita"

24. Take for ___

26. Hon

27. Blood carrier

28. French tale

29. Sponges

30. Beats it

31. the Algonquian language spoken by the Ojibwa

32. 1980s hairstyle with a long strand in the back

33. Fine-tunes

35. One out?

37. On one's back

38. Radiant

39. sorting and allocating aid on the basis of need for or likely benefit from medical treatment or food

40. Ran out

42. 1972 Elton John hit

43. Pet protection org.

45. "___ Dinah" (Frankie Avalon hit)

46. Daly of "Judging Amy"

48. Mid-6th-century date

Across

1. Person from Santa Cruz or San Jos

11. Tiny fraction of a min.

15. Misogynous

16. "Summer and Smoke" heroine

17. a country in northwestern Africa with a provisional military government

18. Brandy flavor

19. "A Nightmare on ___ Street"

20. Collect

21. A deadly sin

22. Civil War side

24. Hammer part

25. "Beloved" heroine

26. "Sunflowers" setting

28. "La la" preceder

29. Battle site in "Animal Farm"

30. Fortifies

32. Austrian composer of waltzes (1804-1849)

34. 100 cents

36. Benjamin Disraeli, e.g.

37. Blocks

40. Talk of the town?

44. ___ throat

45. Rocker Garcia, informally

47. Main impact

48. Brings (out)

49. Chick's sound

51. One-quintillionth: Prefix

52. "Charles in Charge" star

53. the presence of pus-forming bacteria or their toxins in the blood or tissues

55. Cyclades island

56. Three-time speed skating gold medalist Karin

57. Seconds

59. June 6, 1944

60. Slightest traces

61. "___ quam videri" (North Carolina's motto)

62. It drops on the way home

Down

1. Kodaks, e.g.

2. Ready for trouble

3. an unintentional but embarrassing blunder

4. French shooting match

5. Not care ___ for

6. Draw upon again

7. Eastern hospice

8. Packing crew

9. Drive off

10. Warm, so to speak

11. Highest point in Italy?

12. Investigators

13. Parentheses alternatives

14. Hauled

23. Concur

25. Sacred beetle of ancient Egypt

27. Declines

31. Mr., abroad

33. 50 Cent piece

35. Oscar winner of 1990

37. Leaves in the lurch

38. Triumvirates

39. Enters via osmosis

41. 1994 Red Hot Chili Peppers album

42. Altogether

43. Newsman John

44. Canonized monk who introduced the custom of dating events from the birth of Christ

46. Descend again

50. Ski trail

53. Back talk

54. Ado

58. Priestly garb

Puzzle #14
Organizations Doing Important Work

Across

1. Seconds

11. Puccini soprano

15. Top dog

16. a primeval Egyptian personification of air and breath

17. Homey's acceptance

18. Flock member

19. Bones, anatomically

20. "It's Too Late Now" autobiographer

22. Wing, say

26. Code-cracking org.

27. Mormons, initially

28. Low stools

32. Change, as a clock

34. A shrug, verbalized

35. Leave ___ (be permanently damaging)

36. Govt. initiative

37. ___ throat

39. Auto racer Yarborough

40. Lap dogs

42. Breed of large wiry-coated terrier bred in Yorkshire

44. January in Guadalajara

45. They hang around

46. Blackguard

47. Wine: Prefix

49. Escape, in a way

50. Not recognizable by

52. They may be full of gas

56. Actress Talbot

57. Nuclear power

62. Lennon's in-laws

63. Hear something about

64. Mysterious: Var.

65. One-way flights?

Down

1. Mock phrase of insight

2. Adjusts, as a clock

3. a respiratory disease of unknown etiology that apparently originated in mainland China in 2003

4. Philosopher

5. "___ Cried" (1962 hit)

6. "Sesame Street" watcher

7. Mandela's org.

8. A.T.M. maker

9. "Jeopardy!" phrase

10. Bubbly drinks

11. Anklebones

12. Modest

13. One who knows the value of a dollar

14. a woman ancestor

21. hare-like rodent of the pampas of Argentina

23. Self: Prefix

24. Bothers

25. Unwritten reminders

28. 1811 battle site

29. a catecholamine secreted by the adrenal medulla in response to stress (trade name Adrenalin)

30. Nicholson role in "Wolf"

31. "Flying Down ___" (1933 movie)

33. a steep artificial slope in front of a fortification

38. Red Rose, once

41. Sometime today, say

43. Sandra of "Gidget"

48. French story

51. "Duck soup!"

53. Mars: Prefix

54. Borodin's "Prince ___"

55. O.E.D. listings

58. Like some stocks, for short

59. Kid's cry

60. "___ say!"

61. Actress Vardalos of "My Big Fat Greek Wedding"

Puzzle #15
Tickle My Nostrils

Across

1. Kings' milieu

10. Cold sorrel soup

15. any member of the genus Paramecium

16. Bing, bang or boom

17. Was a sounding board

18. Beast of Borden

19. Buy-one-get-one-free item?

20. Some mouths

21. "Carmen" highlight

24. Bloviates

28. Binding

32. Beat

33. Like some agreements

34. Ancient reveler's "whoopee!"

35. Lets go

36. Heavy metal band with the triple-platinum album "Out of the Cellar"

37. Checks

39. Aquarium fish

40. Perfume quantity

41. Shot putter?

42. Fiddled (with)

44. a town in southwest Georgia

47. How many teens go to movies

52. Thomas of "That Girl"

53. someone who attacks

55. "Farewell, mon ami"

56. Place for a road sign

57. Clairvoyants

58. Frets (over)

Down

1. They're over specialists: Abbr.

2. Hic, ___, hoc

3. About

4. College entrance exams

5. In one's cups

6. Racing jibs

7. Biting

8. "Mamma ___!"

9. Ring bearer, maybe

10. Pooh-pooh

11. descended from a common ancestor but through different lines

12. H.S. subject

13. ___ Minor

14. Flashed signs

20. Cézanne contemporary

22. Property recipient, at law

23. "Frasier" character

24. Alamogordo's county

25. Split

26. Became an issue

27. Dry

29. Heavens: Prefix

30. 4:1, e.g.

31. First name in rock

33. Building block

35. Backside

38. Catastrophic

39. Pops

41. Kind of seat

43. Parks and others

44. Latin 101 verb

45. Put on board, as cargo

46. Cheese on crackers

48. "___ fair in love and war"

49. Detective, at times

50. Female suffix

51. Increase, with "up"

53. Communication for the deaf: Abbr.

54. Put away

Puzzle #16
Dealership Secrets

1	2	3	4	5	6	7		8	9	10	11	12	13	14
15								16						
17								18						
19						20	21			22				
23				24						25				
26				27						28				
29			30					31						
	32	33						34			35	36		
		37			38	39	40				41		42	
43	44	45			46					47				
48					49					50				
51					52				53					
54				55			56	57						
58							59							
60							61							

Across

1. Salts

8. Ushers after intermission

15. Calm

16. Hyundai model

17. Lab tube

18. Request to a dealer

19. Advances

20. Not just "a"

22. Kid's name

23. Cries of discovery

24. Feng ___

25. "Steady ___ goes"

26. Hair goops

27. Before: Abbr.

28. French romantic writer (1766-1817)

29. His "4" was retired

30. Revolt

32. More tender

34. Bridget Fonda, to Jane

37. Delighted

41. Egg cells

43. Clear, as a disk

46. Elliptical

47. Bogus

48. Crows' homes

49. High spots

50. Elizabeth of "La Bamba"

51. Spanish houses

52. Barley bristle

53. Buenos ___

54. Blanket

56. Sway

58. wipe away

59. Kind of fair

60. Tried

61. someone who rejects the established culture

Down

1. a hard green Swiss cheese made with skim-milk curd and flavored with clover

2. Insults

3. Beseech

4. Chucks

5. Feed bag contents

6. Clock std.

7. Transparent, modern-style

8. Get

9. an extreme leftist terrorist group formed in Greece in 1971 to oppose the military junta that ruled Greece from 1967 to 1974

10. Like some humor

11. Volunteer

12. Mother of Xerxes I

13. Emergency surgery, for short

14. Helmsley and others

21. Colors

24. Wrangles

30. Essential

31. Dye-yielding shrubs

33. Stop on the way

35. Understandable

36. Fade away

38. Smashed

39. Acknowledge

40. Sully

42. One into collecting

43. Make secret

44. Splits, old-style

45. Holdings

47. Skyline parts

53. "You're ___, ya know that?": Archie Bunker

55. Big: Abbr.

57. AT&T competitor

Puzzle #17
Name that Explorer!

1	2	3	4	5	6	7			8	9	10	11	
12						13		14					15
16								17					
18				19			20			21			
22		23		24				25		26			
27				28		29				30			
		31		32				33					
34	35	36					37						
38						39							
40					41			42		43	44	45	
46			47				48		49				
50		51		52				53		54			
55			56			57			58				
59						60							
	61						62						

Across

1. Noted painter of American rural life

8. Explorer Vasco da ___

12. Put on again, as weight

14. Esoteric

16. Exactly 3 hours for a marathon, e.g.

17. Enter en masse

18. Little bird

19. a mass of ice and snow that permanently covers a large area of land (e.g., the polar regions or a mountain peak)

21. Oil source

22. Parmenides' home

24. Signs up

26. Domingo, e.g.

27. U.S. Open champ, 1985-87

29. A long television program, esp. one to raise funds for charity

31. Adjust, as laces

33. Bullfight attendants

34. Home of Carthage College

37. Site of some bombers

38. Kay Thompson character

39. Attach

40. Dude

42. "Camelot" composer

46. Attention-getter

47. Bantu language

49. ___ Fox

50. Boarding spots: Abbr.

52. Absorbed, in a way

54. Hosp. area

55. Jot

57. Bedtime drink

59. the organ of sight

60. Souvenir shop item

61. Caught in the act

62. They're short on T's

Down

1. Humperdinck heroine

2. Bad-mouth

3. Threshold for the Vienna Boys' Choir

4. Masefield play "The Tragedy of ___"

5. South American monkey

6. Chilled

7. Madness

8. Miracle-___

9. "We'll tak ___ o' kindness yet"

10. Soccer great Diego

11. Oily liquids used in dyemaking

13. Dictate

14. Symbol of Americanism

15. All together

20. "You've got mail" co.

23. Canny

25. Unsaturated alcohol

28. Inferior

30. Associate

32. Things to follow

34. Maintains, as a schedule

35. Stretchables

36. Start of a quote

37. Hangs on the line

39. Letter

41. Dumfries denial

43. 13th-century king of Denmark

44. Concerned ones' assurance

45. Goes off

48. A rival

51. Surprise

53. "Just hear ___ sleigh bells jingling

56. ___ Tha ("The King and I" role)

58. Not just "a"

Puzzle #18
What Colors Mean

Across

1. 19th dynasty's founder

8. deprive through death

15. Tony Manhattan eatery

16. L. M. Montgomery book "Anne of ___"

17. move back and forth very rapidly

18. Honkers

19. Decorating do-overs, for short

20. Contract negotiator: Abbr.

22. Blue eyes or baldness, e.g.

23. an Eskimo hut

24. Red Rose, once

25. Can't help but

26. Vivacious wit

27. Architect William Van ___

28. Chipped in

29. "My boy"

30. of or relating to or denoting the first period of the Mesozoic era

32. Arrangements

34. Colgate rival

37. Construction crew

41. Some Caltech grads, for short

43. Deprive of courage

46. "Alfred" composer

47. Motorists' clubs, in brief

48. ___-foot oil

49. Baptism, for one

50. Partner of rules, slangily

51. Lizard: Prefix

52. ___ anglais (English horn)

53. Trauma aftereffects

54. Neighbor of Georgia

56. Magazine sales

58. More swift

59. Curly-haired dogs

60. Blight

61. Lush fabrics

Down

1. Prepares beans in a way

2. Quick movements

3. inject into the vein

4. Not participate in

5. Tolkien creatures

6. "Comprende?"

7. Nazareth native

8. Fastens (down)

9. Bolivian president Morales

10. Thin hairlike outgrowth of an epidermal cell just behind the tip; absorbs nutrients from the soil

11. Beguile

12. N.Y. Yankees div.

13. Cin

14. Best Director of 1992 and 2004

21. Drink with dim sum

24. Analyze, in a way

30. Gets acquainted with something good

31. a sloping mass of loose rocks at the base of a cliff

33. Sources of a cosmetics oil

35. Coastal flier

36. Shade lighter than palmetto

38. Auto maintenance

39. Beethoven's "Archduke ___"

40. Catches

42. 1973 Man turn cobra movie

43. Risky

44. Almost

45. River through Toledo, Ohio

47. Game keeper?

53. Advance, slangily

55. Occupational ending

57. ___ 180

Puzzle #19
Creators and Their Creations

1	2	3	4	5	6	7		8	9	10	11	12	13	14
15								16						
17							18							
19					20						21			
22					23						24			
25			26		27			28		29				
30				31			32		33					
		34			35									
36	37	38						39			40	41	42	
43				44		45			46					
47				48						49				
50			51		52			53		54				
55			56					57						
58							59							
60							61							

Across

1. outermost layer of the pericarp of fruits as the skin of a peach or grape

8. Unchanged

15. One way to get to work

16. someone employed in a stable to take care of the horses

17. International understanding

19. Singular, to Caesar

20. Hawaiian feasts

21. Opp. of legato, in music

22. Fort Worth sch.

23. "Andy Capp" cartoonist Smythe

24. M.D.'s specialty

25. Quite

27. Ottoman title

29. Eye, at the Eiffel Tower

30. Bring back to domestication

32. Bartender?

34. Celeb

36. Deem

39. "Yea, verily"

43. Beliefs

44. Bartender on TV's Pacific Princess

46. Lentil, e.g.

47. "___ Maria"

48. Addition

49. "Once in Love With ___"

50. Football linemen

52. In-box contents

54. "Jake's Thing" author

55. Slots

58. Arrived quietly

59. "I've been framed!"

60. "First ..."

61. the trait of keeping things secret

Down

1. Muscle that rotates a part outward

2. Dash

3. confer a trust upon

4. Soup or salad ingredient

5. Get an ___ (ace)

6. a unit of weight used in some Moslem countries near the Mediterranean

7. the thin serous membrane around the lungs and inner walls of the chest

8. Mind set?

9. ___ de combat

10. Either of two books of the Apocrypha: Abbr.

11. Boonies

12. Group for young people coping with parental substance abuse

13. One-named 1970's singer

14. Straight

18. Possible source of salmonella poisoning

26. Havens

27. Brand of cola

28. Heirloom location

29. Gold braid

31. Greek letters

33. ___ grass

35. Right of passage

36. Not for free

37. 53 minutes past the hour

38. Sound systems

40. Mariner's measure

41. of or relating to the group of Semitic languages

42. Amazing adventure

45. Covers

51. Preserve, in a way

52. Arabic for "commander"

53. When repeated, like some shows

54. Jewish month

56. "Bad Behavior" star, 1993

57. a committee in the executive branch of government that advises the president on foreign and military and national security

Puzzle #20
Holy Stories

Across

1. Card game played to 61

12. Gas additive brand

15. any joyous diversion

16. Altar constellation

17. Flips

19. The Santa

20. Dist. around

21. Huffing and puffing

22. Up to the job

23. Hockey's Phil

25. Sinn

27. Locale for a vision of the Apostle Paul

29. Actor Connery

30. Most impertinent

32. Charlotte Gainsbourg's father

33. Extinct New Zealand flock

34. 'This ___ outrage!'

36. Egyptian king credited with founding the First Dynasty

39. a rough and bitter manner

43. Actor Sharif

44. They get a licking

45. Fasten on

47. "Hey Jude" chorus

49. Potentially treacherous driving surface

50. 32,000 ounces

51. Launch platform

54. Stow, as cargo

55. Some old syrups

58. Mel the slugger

59. Kitchen vessels

60. Irish Sea feeder

61. County ENE of San Francisco

Down

1. a poor golf stroke in which the club head hits the ground before hitting the ball

2. Showy bloomers

3. Ancient region of France

4. DJ Rick who owns rick.com

5. This is only a test org.

6. Biter in a swamp

7. Emporio ___

8. Sound systems

9. Grafton's ___ for Innocent

10. Restaurant policy, sometimes

11. Bridge bid, briefly

12. More mushy

13. Arboreal marker

14. Series opener

18. French composer best remembered for his pop operas (1842-1912)

24. Punch ingredient?

26. able to understand and use numbers

27. Actress Carrere

28. Journalist James

31. 1980s sitcom star, familiarly

32. Part of UCSD

35. Rds.

36. Camera or gun holder

37. Spring (from)

38. Fabray of TV fame

40. Three-syllable foot, in poetry

41. Weeks in Madrid

42. Master-to-be

44. Playground retort

46. Black Sea port

48. Like much ethnic humor

52. Purim's month

53. Merrill of the movies

54. Slimming surgery

56. Peak, for short

57. Atlanta-based health agcy

Puzzle #21
Religious Celebrations

Across

1. "It will come ___ surprise"

5. Least bit

8. Discontinue

12. A bit thick

14. Oscar winner for "West Side Story"

16. Deli order

17. (of snakes and eels) naturally footless

18. a list of acknowledgements of those who contributed to the creation of a film (usually run at the end of the film)

19. Passes unnoticed

20. "Belling the Cat" author

21. Celebrated St. Patrick's Day

22. Firstborn

25. ___ vie

27. Shoot-'em-up

31. When doubled, a Pacific capital

32. "___ Maria"

33. Tardy person's query

35. "In the Good Old Summertime" lyricist Shields

36. Congo river

38. Hail

40. Garbage

42. Ancient ascetic

43. Moguls

45. Actor Davis

49. Haloes

50. Service aces?

52. For money

53. Back doors

54. Rots

55. Chinese restaurant offering

56. 1914 battle line

57. John, Paul and George: Abbr.

58. Delhi wrap

Down

1. Pet protection org.

2. Gawk

3. Honkers

4. Beats

5. Decree

6. Doctrines

7. Phone trio

8. Enlarged letter at the start of a chapter

9. Site of many military parades

10. With limited funds

11. Cal ___

13. Not quite in the majors

14. Washington locale, with "the"

15. Express

19. Persian governors

21. Futile

23. At home, to Hadrian

24. Lacking vigor

26. A long, long time

27. ___ monde

28. Hints

29. Track event

30. Suit to ___

34. The U.S., to Mexicans

37. Infamous Colombian drug lord

39. Cuts

41. Dearest

44. Feed bag contents

46. A bit, colloquially

47. ___ tube

48. Assignment in une

49. United States showman famous for his Wild West Show (1846-1917)

50. After-dinner drink

51. "___ Death" (Grieg work)

53. Some film ratings

Across

1. marked or decorated with stripes

8. 451, in old Rome

12. Linguistically groundbreaking

14. Dash

16. Restrained

17. Strictly in the style of

18. Some mdse. from Amazon.com

19. Celtics head coach, 1995-97

21. Former Utah senator Jake

22. Business letter abbr.

24. Singer O'Connor

26. ___-relief

27. Conundrum

29. Deli slice

31. With regret

33. Whine and cry

34. Critter

37. They're blue, in rhyme

38. Narrow bodies

39. Teeth: Prefix

40. Create a disturbance

42. Make into law

46. Canadian pop star Gryner

47. Band-leading Tommy

49. Blender setting

50. Dutch artist Jan van der ___, who painted landscapeS

52. Triangular sail

54. MGM motto word

55. Ocean current

57. Pikes

59. Volleyball position

60. "Hmmm ..."

61. Q followers

62. Samaritans

Down

1. Moviegoer's chocolate bite

2. Care for

3. Ribs ... or ribbings

4. Under the weather

5. 'Jabberwocky,' e.g.

6. French peers

7. Adherent

8. Red Cross course, briefly

9. Narcotic

10. Rest on top of

11. Corporate web

13. "Spider Baby" star, 1964

14. Prepares for a rough ride

15. They may be taken out

20. Agent

23. Headlands

25. Signify

28. Squealed

30. Making steam

32. Bruise

34. Ancient galleys

35. Peter Carl Fabergé, at times

36. Nourishing noshes

37. Like most modern furniture

39. Opposite of proximal, in anatomy

41. Altar constellation

43. Say, boss, how about ___?

44. Rush headlong

45. The girl in "Working Girl," and others

48. ___ come

51. 'Hud' director Martin

53. Fictional son of a rajah

56. Noted 'krautrock' band

58. The R of Roy G. Biv

Puzzle #23
On the Road to Recovery

Across

1. Parodies

8. Recovered from a bad stroke, say

15. In no hurry

16. A Greek restaurant

17. a transcription from one alphabet to another

19. 'The Lion King' heroine

20. Rhubarb

21. Siberian city

22. Attached to (prefix)

23. Bright, to Brecht

24. Linguistic suffix on tax

25. Direction for cooking tuna

27. Birds that talk back

29. Weekend lead-ins (abbr.)

30. Obdurate

32. Can't turn away from

34. Gunpowder component

36. UnScramble this Word: t n a l p e a a

39. Internet domains: identify the country: il

43. "___ pronounce you man and wife"

44. Ranee's raiment

46. what is the capital of norway

47. What word links above, crew, glass

48. Of what is pekoe a variety

49. Part of a década

50. Breed of horse

52. Reach in amount

54. Grasp intuitively

55. Judges the crying of comic Johnson?

58. Quality Bono and Cher share

59. 1942 Abbott and Costello movie

60. 1973 man-becomes-cobra movie

61. No longer iffy

Down

1. Relevance

2. fortification consisting of a low wall

3. And other women: Lat.

4. Baby Names Beginning With "R": Meaning: Catherine

5. Plural -y

6. Requests for developers: Abbr.

7. covered with an adhesive material

8. Zinc ___ (ointment ingredient)

9. Heavenly string

10. Baby Names Beginning With "O": Meaning: Egg

11. Fasten on

12. Base coats

13. Inability to smell

14. Most foul

18. Useless Trivia: Spiders have _____ blood.

26. Further shorten, maybe

27. 'Black Velvet' singer Alannah

28. Composer Erik

29. Iron prefix

31. Back muscle

33. Mis' neighbors

35. Sheet music notations

36. Vagabonds

37. Frogs and toads

38. Jots down

40. Thin ___

41. Goal of some Río Bravo crossers

42. Appear mopey

45. Diners

51. ___ Chili Bowl (historic D.C. restaurant)

52. Broadsides

53. Toddler's attire

54. Frobe who played Goldfinger

56. what did david stirling found

57. Preschooler

Puzzle #24
Scene of the Crime

1	2	3	4	■	5	6	7	■	■	■	8	9	10	11
12				13					■	14	15			
16								■	17					
18							■	19						
20					■		21							■
■			22		23	24				■	25			26
27	28	29							30	■	31			
32			■	33						34	■	35		
36			37	■	38						39			
40				41	■	42					■	■	■	■
■	43				44			■		45		46	47	48
49						■	50	51						
52					■	53								
54					■	55								
56				■	57			■	58					

Across

1. Classic cars

5. Realize

8. Forensics team (abbr.)

12. Collared one

14. a genus of Strigidae

16. Race line-up

17. Addition symbols?

18. "The Alchemist" painter

19. Tycoons' holdings

20. Famed 'Titanic' casualty

21. Brie, Camembert, etc.

22. Not aching

25. Condition

27. 'Einstein on the Beach Trying to Score Some Heroin,' e.g.?

31. Anthem-starting words

32. Seam stuff

33. Bancs

35. Suffix with Capri

36. Support systems, of a sort

38. "The Three Musketeers" actress, 1948

40. Shout to dog

42. 'Thy Neighbor's Wife' author

43. Harvest-time collection

45. Humane org.

49. British V.I.P.'s, to Brits

50. Remote, for one

52. Italian astronomer Giovanni Battista ___, after whom a comet is named

53. Battered and sautéed in butter

54. Was caught in the rain

55. One who showed up

56. Things on rings

57. Part of UNLV

58. Frobe who played Goldfinger

Down

1. Jamaican figure

2. Some Art Deco pieces

3. Praying figure

4. Solemn

5. Ending for hip or friend (4)

6. Plural suffix with auction

7. Some MIT grads

8. Wrap artist?

9. Get the point

10. Lacking will power

11. Ganja

13. Less forgiving

14. Pinnacle

15. Scotch products

19. Light

21. "Rambo" actor Richard and kin

23. Styx crosser

24. Poppy products

26. Watchful one

27. Fireplace projections

28. fragrant rootstock of various irises especially Florentine iris

29. Access the contents of

30. Commedia dell'__

34. Philosopher Langer

37. Alternates

39. Quiescent

41. Lackluster?

44. Big name in sporting goods

46. Like Oedipus' marriage

47. Apple device

48. On the ball

49. Lead ___ life

50. Govt. job training prog.

51. Inning trio

53. __ de mer

Puzzle #25

See You in Court!

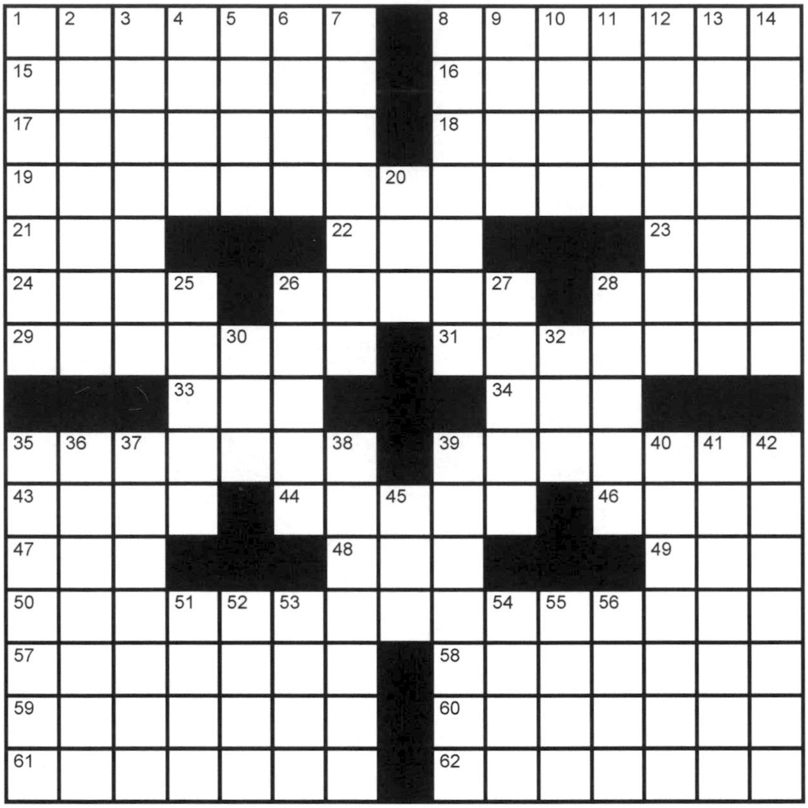

Across

1. Paints the town red

8. Washing machine cycle

15. Common baseball count

16. Carriage part?

17. Really funny

18. Group for young people coping with parental substance abuse

19. Let go

21. Mid-6th-century date

22. Large amount of money

23. Bubkes

24. Noted plus-size model

26. Dad's rival

28. Suit to ___

29. larceny by threat of violence

31. Fleet activities

33. "... ___ mouse?"

34. "Now ___ theater near you!"

35. Handle

39. Proportional

43. Hollywood up-and-comer

44. Crosses over

46. Ado

47. Magazine no.

48. Crumb

49. F.D.R. plan

50. They'll do for now

57. Delta, for one

58. Notify

59. an advanced student or graduate in medicine gaining supervised practical experience (`houseman' is a British term)

60. One offering a sales incentive

61. St. Francis ___ (French prelate)

62. Daggers

Down

1. a pupil who lives at school during term time

2. San ___, Marin County

3. Go over again

4. Aesop's also-ran

5. Draftable

6. Modern electronic organizers, for short

7. By fair means or foul

8. Manners

9. Anger, with "up"

10. Old musical notes

11. Actor Green of "Buffy the Vampire Slayer"

12. City on the Susquehanna

13. a studio especially for an artist or designer

14. Awakens

20. Propel, in a way

25. W.W. II craft

26. Acts the blowhard

27. Combs et al.

28. Military plane acronym

30. "Ol' Rockin' ___" (bin-mate of the 1957 album "Ford Favorites")

32. Confounded

35. "To reiterate ..."

36. "Fear Street" series author

37. Getaway spots

38. Heroic poems

39. Crying

40. Downsize without layoffs

41. Concert recording, e.g.

42. Back-to-school purchases

45. Branch

51. "Guilty," e.g.

52. Demoiselle

53. "Green Gables" girl

54. Adopt-___

55. Passed quickly

56. ___-Altaic languages

Puzzle #26
The Reel Life

Across

1. Marketable securities, e.g.

11. Branch of Islam

15. I'm fining you 2000 Flushes after passing the supermarket; in the future, please follow the ___

16. ___ scale of hardness

17. a kind of thermometer for measuring heat radiation

18. The Santa

19. ___ of reality

20. Empathize

22. Speller's words of clarification

23. Green Mountain Boys leader

27. Bleacher feature

28. Bear young, in the barnyard

29. Now you ___ ...

30. Football Hall-of-Famer Yale ___

31. She, in Rome

32. Weight allowances

33. Magazine department

35. 'A Man Needs ___' (Neil Young song)

39. Word derivation: abbr.

40. Maria on Mars

44. Seal inscription

45. Laughter, in La Mancha

46. Both (Prefix)

47. Bullied

49. Seas (French)

50. Saree-clad royals

51. Marie Osmond's ___ Belle dolls

53. Author Robert __ Butler

54. Answer continued

59. GE Building muralist

60. Listed

61. Swedish actress Persson

62. Permits passage, perhaps

Down

1. 'TV Guide' acronym

2. inability to use or understand language (spoken or written) because of a brain lesion

3. More disreputable

4. a breeding ground for herons

5. Navy VIPs

6. Like some vamps

7. Thimbleful

8. U.K. record label

9. Up to, in short

10. Not easily amused

11. Not so big

12. Dragon's home, in song

13. "Ugh!"

14. Says yes

21. Bridge positions

22. Delta hub's code

24. Mosaic piece

25. Tackles the issue

26. Break down, to a Brit

33. Photoshop creator

34. Flows forth

35. Bierce the cynic

36. Esai of 'NYPD Blue'

37. Yom Kippur observers

38. Mark your card!

40. Indian pastries

41. Some retired profs

42. Worn down

43. Nickname inappropriate for an only child

48. Sassy consonants

52. Kidvid explorer

55. What's made on principal?: Abbr

56. Ascribable (to)

57. Akihito's title: Abbr

58. Dutch city

Across

1. Part of a Spanish play

5. 'The Last Puritan' family

11. Lobbying org.

14. Catfish Row woman

15. Attacks

16. After

17. Many a Twitter message

19. Celtic god of the sea

20. Spanish pronoun

21. Behind

23. Homesteaders

26. Having feeling

27. Valets, at times

29. Becomes established

30. Messy places

32. Brinker in stories

33. A person who was of great standards. Has done some thing well, or pleased some one.

38. Holy Hindu figure

39. 'Stormy Weather' star Lena

40. Serengeti herd

43. Can't turn away from

48. Issued

50. Suddenly spook

51. All tangled up

53. A chorus line?

54. Mich. city that's lost half its population in the past fifty years

55. Mike Ditka, e.g.?

58. Vane dir.

59. Fleece providers

60. Cataract site

61. Sound from a flat

62. Abhor

63. Six-foot vis-

Down

1. Swarm

2. Ceremonial burner

3. Fly with a bad bite

4. Natives of the Caucasus

5. Once more: Abbr.

6. Batch

7. Homeowner's paper

8. Slaves to crosswords?

9. Buttonmakers' materials

10. Tristram Shandy's creator

11. Visibly scared out of one's wits

12. a warning serves to make you more alert to danger

13. Drives recklessly

18. Early capital of Macedonia

22. ... that   question

24. Soaks flax

25. unscramble h a i r s

28. Liliaceous plants

31. Classifies

33. a state of robust good health

34. Flows forth

35. Desires

36. Go ___ some length

37. lower the rated electrical capability of electrical apparatus

38. Dwells

41. Kiefer's dad

42. Ripe for a trial lawyer

44. Off the mark

45. Bowls

46. Genotype determinant

47. One without scissors, perhaps

49. One may go to the dogs

52. Not at all clever

56. Orientation week figures, for short

57. Mil. amphibian

Puzzle #28
Famous as a Group

Across

1. Best Actor of 1967

8. D and C, in D.C.

15. Extra

16. "Drive" pop group

17. Composer Dvorak

18. Bolsters the confidence of

19. Freshest stories?

21. Part of "D.A.": Abbr.

22. Suffix with ether

23. TV drama settings

24. Drink with dim sum

26. Scottish hillsides

28. Some health info ads, for short

29. Sweet-talks

31. Abominates

33. "___ Boot"

34. Coolers, briefly

35. First-aid equipment

39. James I and Charles I

43. "Iliad" warrior

44. of or relating to or characteristic of Scotland or its people or culture or its English dialect or Gaelic language

46. Escape, in a way

47. All the rage

48. "Isn't ___ bit like you and me?" (Beatles lyric)

49. the syllable naming the sixth (submediant) note of a major or minor scale in solmization

50. "Listen!"

57. Prepares for a second printing

58. Animal, to granny

59. Science for farmers

60. Diner sign

61. Oceanographic charts

62. Everything, to a lyricist

Down

1. Prison camps

2. Small, simple flute

3. Not exact

4. NYSE banner events

5. "Look Homeward, Angel" hero Eugene

6. (Greek mythology) goddess of discord

7. Many cottage dwellers

8. Not going anywhere

9. "Just hear ___ sleigh bells jingling

10. Medical advice, often

11. Its cap. is Quito

12. lacking external ears

13. Small, furry African climber

14. 1973 man-becomes-cobra movie

20. This may give you gas: Abbr.

25. Some German exports

26. Conquers

27. an area that includes places where several people can sit

28. Former European money

30. airtight sealed metal container for food or drink or paint etc.

32. Fort Worth sch.

35. Vast arid wastes

36. a person who receives support and protection from an influential patron who furthers the protege's career

37. It's typed with the left pinkie

38. Breaks

39. Positions

40. connected by kinship, common origin, or marriage

41. Flirts

42. Domains of influence

45. Antipoverty agcy.

51. Biblical land

52. the Babylonian goddess of the watery deep and daughter of Ea

53. 'Vette feature, perhaps

54. a small vehicle with four wheels in which a baby or child is pushed around

55. ___ fire (started burning something)

56. People: Prefix

Puzzle #29
European Go-Tos

Across

1. Color Me ___, 1990s R&B group

5. "Thou ___, most ignorant monster": Shak.

10. Spun platters

13. North Carolina county

14. Floral essential oil

15. One in attendance

16. Greeting from a dwarf?

18. Madrid month

19. Always, in verse

20. Den ___ (Dutch city, to the Dutch)

21. Takes in, perhaps

23. *Not so important

26. Bacteriologist known for his dish

27. Fix, as a bow

30. Picked new straws, say

32. Is rife

33. Punjabi breakfast beverage

36. Chills and fever cause

38. "Happy Days" character

39. Followed obediently

41. Shady strolling spots

43. Irish lullaby syllables

46. Saucer-eyed Broadway star

49. Digs in the Alps

51. Commedia dell'__

52. Unkempt hair, maybe

53. Disraeli's title

54. Excites

57. Prepares prunes

58. Rodents, jocularly

59. Coca-Cola founder Candler and politician Hutchinson

60. Spanish letter after "ka"

61. High-altitude home

62. Ganja

Down

1. Rhine River city

2. Answer to the folk riddle "Over the hills, over the hills / Goes a fur coat"

3. Long-shot candidate

4. Etym.

5. Save for later

6. ___ an accident!

7. Knicknack rack

8. Spend less money, in store names

9. Halloween bagful

10. More isolated

11. Duke or earl

12. Hit show signs

15. Sense

17. "Everything is going to be okay ..."

22. Tots

24. Easy-park shopping places

25. Person after a lifestyle change, self-descriptively

28. Application-form abbr.

29. Brownie's org.

31. Racer Bobby

33. Event for Trisha Y.

34. Shakespearean prince

35. Menu option

37. Utterly lost

40. Slipper?

42. Sit in jail

44. having a surface covered with a network of cracks and small crevices

45. a genus of tropical American plants have sword-shaped leaves and a fleshy compound fruits composed of the fruits of several flowers (such as pineapples)

47. Poet who wrote "I have executed a memorial longer lasting than bronze"

48. ___ Porridge hot

49. Cuisine mushroom

50. Salute

55. 'Kill Bill' tutor Pai ___

56. "___ in Icarus" (1979 French thriller)

Across

1. a volcano in the Andes in Chile

7. Secure

14. Rubbernecking

15. ... city?

16. Actress North

17. Field work

18. "Jewel Song," e.g., in "Faust"

20. John, Paul and George: Abbr.

21. Ticks off

22. Southern breakfast dish

23. Obi accessory

24. Some Caltech grads, for short

25. Shopping meccas

26. being or from or characteristic of another place or part of the world

27. Gurus

28. Inclination

29. Gofers

30. Special team

31. Actress Kruger and others

32. Entry in a spaceship log

33. Brighton baby buggies

34. Runner Nurmi, the Flying Finn

35. Brit. money

38. "and other things"

39. Fin dc ___ (remainder): Fr.

40. footwear shaped to fit the foot (below the ankle) with a flexible upper of leather or plastic and a sole and heel of heavier material

41. Doc bloc

42. Today's teens

44. an eastern French region rich in iron-ore deposits

46. a port city in western France on the Loire estuary

47. Becomes twisted

48. It may be blacked out

49. BBQ annoyance

50. a female person who is a fellow member of a sorority or labor union or other group

Down

1. a girl or young woman who is unmarried

2. towards the shore from the water

3. Much Mongolian geography

4. "It Must Be Him" singer and others

5. Length x width, for a rectangle

6. Fights again

7. Newspaper section

8. Singer Amos and others

9. capital and largest city of Italy

10. Letters before a name

11. Cousins of carrots

12. Where K-I-S-S-I-N-G happens

13. "Rob Roy" star, 1995

15. Garden pests

19. The wreath, or chaplet, surmounting or encircling the helmet of a knight and bearing the crest

23. Defeatist's words

25. "___ the sea and wind when both contend": "Hamlet"

26. ___ the good

27. Quarterback Phil

28. Colonial captives

29. Menu option

30. Deborah of "Days of Our Lives"

31. First N.F.L. player to rccord 100 receptions in a season

32. Allahabad attire

33. Family of 18th- and 19th-century painters

34. Writer

35. Tried to bring down

36. Language sound unit

37. a spring that discharges hot water and steam

39. Angler's gear

40. Turns state's evidence

42. Bearing

43. Rikki-Tikki-___

45. Literary monogram

Puzzle #31
Opera Populaire

Across

1. Cause for carrying an inhaler

7. Subject of this puzzle

14. Sugary foods

15. Frequent Errol Flynn co-star whose son played Gilligan's skipper on TV

16. European capital

17. Atoll bought by Brando

18. "Idylls of the King" character

19. Drunkards

21. "60 Minutes" regular

22. Rules, for short

23. "Don't Cry for Me, Argentina" musical

25. Barber's job

26. U.S. ___

27. Song ender

28. Letter-shaped construction pieces

30. Name of two German saints

32. More authentic

34. Flush

36. Exact

40. Like Chippendale furniture

42. Gland: Prefix

43. Suited for high schoolers, on video game packaging

46. Cries of discovery

48. A hand

49. "The Dukes of Hazzard" spinoff

50. Other women, in Oaxaca

52. "___ quam videri" (North Carolina's motto)

53. "Snowy" bird

55. Amerada ___ (Fortune 500 company)

56. "___ Death" (Grieg work)

57. Backside

59. "Dixie" composer

61. Lift

62. Reason to close up shop

63. CDC member?

64. Back-talker

Down

1. Invited a lady to the Flower Ball?

2. H1N1, more commonly

3. 'Young Frankenstein' actress

4. Flip response?

5. Atlas abbr.

6. How matching items are sold

7. Sanctified

8. ___ grass

9. Cuckoos

10. Broken to bits

11. 'Boom-de-ay' lead-in

12. God, in the Old Testament

13. Spheres

15. Clothing

20. Cook too long

24. "___ want for Christmas ..."

27. New England catch

29. Greek letters

31. Set aside

33. Warm welcomes

35. Opposite of endo-

37. Evaluate anew

38. Cordial

39. Guide

41. Calling

43. Thatched

44. Pier of "The Silver Chalice"

45. Spanish constructions

47. Gauge

51. Pang

52. Chair designer Charles

54. CREF's partner

58. Aliens, for short

60. "Mamma ___!"

Puzzle #32
Industrial Tools

1	2	3	4	5	6	7			8	9	10	11	12
13								14	15				
16								17					
18			19		20					21			
22		23		24				25					
26			27		28			29					
30				31		32	33						
		34		35									
36	37	38						39		40	41	42	
43					44	45	46						
47			48			49	50						
51			52				53		54				
55		56				57		58					
59						60							
61						62							

Across

1. Vitally important

8. Shears for metal

13. Dorky

14. Quaint sandlot game

16. Actress Arquette

17. Old Buick model

18. From ___ Z

19. Chapel in the Vatican

21. Mixologist's workplace

22. ___ Rebellion (19th-century Rhode Island Republican insurrection)

24. Really big shoe

25. Course obstacle

26. Tools for duels

28. Nine-digit ID

29. Wojtyla who was John Paul II

30. Marker for some sale items

32. Throttle

34. Now

36. Hooey

39. Morocco seaport

43. Bull shit detectors?

44. Maw's partner

46. Ridge for climbers

47. Giant Mel et al.

48. Reached, as the truth

50. Working without __

51. Biz bigwig

52. Neuters

54. Asian river, the ___ Darya

55. Luxuriant

57. Join, redundantly

59. Fabray of TV fame

60. Fully grasp

61. Icelandic epics

62. Blocks

Down

1. Showoff

2. Atomic relative

3. Having a bill, as a cap

4. 'Snakes __ Plane'

5. Canterbury cans

6. Broadway moppet

7. Car options

8. Ballesteros of golf

9. 'There's ___ in team ...'

10. Shipping hazard

11. Sun blocker

12. Suddenly spook

14. Sets straight

15. Prime-time hour

20. Make a mosaic

23. New shoots

25. Hunting call

27. Fully fills

29. One of Pooh's pals

31. Main mail HQ

33. 1992 Best Actor nominee

35. Zinger

36. Icy treat

37. Tablet

38. Amaze

40. Old Roman coins

41. List

42. Pulls some strings?

45. Appliers of polish

48. Man at a square dance

49. Belief

52. Hammer and Spade, for example: abbr.

53. Command to Rover

56. Place for grazing

58. Stately tree

Puzzle #33
Hey Sugar!

1	2	3	4	5	6	7	8	9		10	11	12	13	
14										15				16
17										18				
19				20					21					
22			23		24			25						
26				27		28						29		
30					31			32		33	34			
			35						36					
37	38	39				40		41				42	43	44
45					46		47			48				
49			50	51					52		53			
54						55			56			57		
58					59					60				
61					62									
	63				64									

Across

1. After just one look

10. EU member

14. And for dessert, a slice of ___ pie.

15. The results ___

17. Free

18. Too trusting

19. CNN alumnus Dobbs

20. Thumbs-ups

21. Places with French classes

22. Buffalo's county

24. Holds true to one's beliefs

26. Narrates

28. Gaelic

29. Frequent soccer score

30. Sigmoid

32. Trig function

35. 'Platoon' setting

36. C.W. Post is part of it (abbr.)

37. Loser

41. Galway or Calais

45. Irish Sea tourist center (abbr.)

46. Bank posting

48. Hero of a Gluck opera

49. Ranks

53. Three hots and

54. Hollywood's Harvey

55. "Take ___!"

57. Incoming (abbr.)

58. Freud contemporary

59. Get out of the way

61. Ur's land

62. Carrier to E Asia, perhaps

63. Yankees bench coach Tony

64. Tape in advance

Down

1. Supposedly protective items

2. Cassiterite et al

3. 'The Lark' playwright

4. March 2012 ABC debut with Kristin Chenoweth

5. Portrait painter Sir Peter

6. Couturier Hardy

7. Canceled out

8. Salad option

9. Logan abbr.

10. Judges' seats

11. The ___ Good Feelings

12. Crosby hit "Sweet   "

13. Yields

16. Get comfy-cozy

21. English Channel swimmer Gertrude

23. Oxlike antelope

25. U.S. codebreakers

27. Fokker foe

31. Celebrity chef on TV

33. See you in Rome?

34. Old Toyota

37. ___ a dog

38. Stayed out of sight

39. Words after handing over your address (7)

40. Luftwaffe foe

41. 'Now listen ...'

42. A British passenger steamship SS City ____

43. Stock up on again

44. ... where angels fear ___

47. Self-conscious laugh

50. Dutch painter Jan

51. Beatified Junipero

52. Tastiness

56. Have the desired effect

59. Gullible one

60. Debs, e.g.: Abbr

Puzzle #34
Winners

Across

1. Turner et al.

6. Pie Pageant winner?

15. Here and there

16. 'Fame' singer

17. Capone's successor

18. Sing in court

19. Doo follower

20. Easter tone

22. __ dixit (assertion)

23. Toledo zoo animal?

24. 1967 Oscar winner Parsons

26. Sound from a flat

27. Civil rights scholar/activist Guinier

29. Glockenspiel cousin

31. Discharge

32. Jazz trombonist Edward "Kid" __

33. Chaplin persona

37. Attacks

39. Less dull

40. Acid-base reaction products

41. Scanning resolution meas

43. Madrid movie

44. 'There Will Be Blood' site

47. Latin 101 word

48. ___-jongg

51. Tidies

53. Suffix with Capri

54. Byron's daughter and others

56. Rydell High musical

57. Part of UCSD

58. Holds back

60. Qatari or Kuwaiti leaders

62. Chat

63. 'Pick someone else!'

64. Got behind

65. Chasm

Down

1. Spider-Man's favorite brand of butter?

2. Capital where Polynesian Airlines is headquartered

3. Twice Told Tales writer, with 70 Across

4. Best Play after 'The Last Night of Ballyhoo'

5. Michael of R.E.M.

6. Cathedral

7. Like mad?

8. Mother of Dionysus

9. Fishhook attachments

10. Hexadecimal A

11. Berry in some recently-disputed diets

12. Pike entryways

13. Head lock

14. Enclosures to eds.

21. Tie at the racetrack?

25. Back of a kitchen?

28. '___ be expected...'

30. Betel nut tree

34. Hostility

35. Soldiers

36. Masks

38. Speller's words of clarification

39. Firing sites

41. Tension-relaxing time

42. Gratified

45. Smooth, in a score

46. Less heedless

48. Exchanges

49. Take ___ breath

50. Must

52. ...like you've ghost

55. British submachine gun

59. Orientation week figures, for short

61. Word with angry or flash

Puzzle #35
Work through Abbreviations

Across

1. Gospel writer

11. Abbr. with a date

15. Puppet

16. Elisabeth in 'Cocktail'

17. Eloquent

18. A whole slew

19. Backsplash makeup

20. Edinburgh exclamation

21. Perpetual, in poetry

23. Some MIT grads

24. Jai follower

25. Peak

26. Dutch painter Jan

28. Certain Prot.

30. Land in the Seine

31. Main vertical lines on graphs

33. Fidgety

35. 'It's my turn!'

37. Cosmic exploration org.

38. Asian part of Turkey

42. Old gold coin

45. Auction action

46. Deal breakers

47. Poet Stephen Vincent -

49. Lug

51. Bath bottom?

54. Derisive interjection

55. Born in

56. Rapper Tone-__

57 Top-notch

58. Atmospheric prefix

59. Cartoon bird

62. Best Supporting Actor winner after Buttons

63. Like some suits

64. Protuberance

65. Blanche DuBois's sister

Down

1. Overdoes it onstage

2. A little of this, a little of that

3. Uzbekistan border lake

4. The time of Nick?

5. Viscous stuff

6. Register, as at university

7. Name in cameras

8. More restless

9. Train depot (abbr.)

10. Broadcast

11. Banana oil, e.g.

12. Peewee

13. Goes underground

14. Neuters

22. Scientist's cylinder

24. Aka windflowers

27. Stage direction

29. Foot, in zoology

32. Arias

34. Hair scare

36. Never, in Nuremberg

38. Teetotal

39. Nikita's "never mind"

40. Stuck

41. Happy __

43. It's   guess

44. City near Hackensack

48. ___ was ...

50. Oscar winning actress Rainer

52. Where clowns ride

53. A driver turns it

57. Indigo-dye source

60. - wise guy!

61. __ tree

1	2	3	4	5	6	■	7	8	9	10	11	12	■
13						■	14						15
16					17	18							
19		■	20				■	21					
22		23	■	24			25	■	26				
27			28	■	29			30	■	31			
32			■	33	■	34			35				
■		36		■	37	■	38			■	■	■	
39	40	41				42	■	43			44	45	46
47			■	48			49	■	50				
51		52	■	53				54	■	55			
56			57	■	58				59	■	60		
61				62					63				
64						■	■	65					
■	66					■	■	67					

Across

1. Seal

7. faint and difficult to analyze

13. Just enough to whet one's appetite

14. She never reached Howland Island

16. Normally pricey garment that hardly fazes a wealthy customer

19. Amigo

20. Development developments

21. "___ of Two Cities" (Dickens novel)

22. Above

24. "___ to the Top": Keni Burke song

26. Senegalese-American rapper

27. Explorer Amundsen

29. Ancient African logic game

31. Abbr. on a bank statement

32. Not alfresco

34. Five Nations tribe

36. Da's opposite

38. Song ender

39. Wisconsin city

43. Rubbernecked

47. "C'___ la vie!"

48. "Dagnabbit!"

50. Attendance counter

51. Blues singer James

53. Anklebones

55. Stops: Abbr.

56. Iron

58. Indications

60. Canals, to a Venetian

61. Momentous

64. Clear again

65. Overlay

66. Beloved

67. Gauge

Down

1. Italian aperitif

2. Pigged out

3. a gathering of passengers sufficient to fill an automobile

4. Residence: Abbr.

5. Carve in stone

6. "Coffee, ___ Me?"

7. Congressional periods

8. Detroit org.

9. La ___ Tar Pits

10. 'Is __ fact?'

11. aromatic Turkish tobacco

12. By and by

15. Ridiculous Starbucks size

17. Struck, old-style

18. 1963 song, '__ Fine'

23. the noise of something dropping (as into liquid)

25. Midshipmen's prep program

28. Senior member

30. Humdingers

33. Change, as a clock

35. Mild oaths

37. Clobbered

39. Niobe, e.g.

40. Greek goddess of justice

41. Pronounced

42. Courtyards

44. the radical -NO2 or any compound containing it (such as a salt or ester of nitrous acid)

45. Current events around Christmas

46. Stars and stripes, and others

49. Army N.C.O.

52. Nolan Ryan, notably

54. The "I" in IV

57. ___-Pei (dog)

59. Attends

62. the compass point midway between south and southeast

63. Feed format for blogs

Puzzle #37
Think Like a Student

1	2	3	4	5	6	7		8	9	10	11	12	13	14
15								16						
17								18						
19					20		21				22			
23						24			25					
	26			27	28	29			30					
31							32				33	34	35	
36						37			38					
39				40		41								
		42				43								
44	45	46			47				48			49		
50				51		52	53		54					
55			56			57		58						
59						60								
61						62								

Across

1. Seminole chief

8. Campus life

15. 'Fiddler on the Roof' role

16. "The Plague" setting

17. "Far out!"

18. Joe Bruin and Tommy Trojan

19. Aspiring atty.'s exam

20. Baddies

22. "Song of the South" song syllables

23. Come/ - spell

24. Trying people

26. Changes

30. Apr. addressee

31. Rebels

32. Juilliard deg.

33. Dungeons & Dragons game co.

36. Ballot winner

37. Breathing aid

39. "Absolutely!"

40. Aliens, for short

41. Syndicated, as 'Seinfeld'

42. Breaking capacity, briefly

43. Paraphrase

44. Gave in

48. Inclines

50. Shoe strengthener

51. Accommodate

54. Uma, in "The Producers"

55. Town overlooking Florence

57. Troubles

59. Like leftovers

60. CDC member?

61. Correspondence

62. 1973 man-becomes-cobra movie

Down

1. Milky gems

2. Magazine for neophyte needlepointers?

3. 'All __ Great and Small'

4. Delighted

5. "Look here!"

6. Airport pickup

7. Tap ___ (get the frat party going)

8. Willie of "Eight Is Enough"

9. Ranks

10. Chief prosecutors

11. Rots

12. Chip away at

13. High hat

14. Facilitates

21. ___ gestae

25. Ancient debarkation point

27. Back

28. Dry

29. Go-aheads

31. 180° turn, slangily

32. Filly's mother

33. Burrito wrappers

34. Unable to reach Nod

35. Cabernet, e.g.

38. Breaks

42. Attacks

43. Food stat.

44. Bad

45. Angler's gear

46. Cold shower?

47. Chicago's ___ Expressway

49. MS. enclosures

52. Academic types

53. Mai ___

56. Native: Suffix

58. "Greetings" org.

Puzzle #38
Hosts of TV Shows

Across

1. Buying out the store, maybe

9. Itsy-bitsy bits

14. It's all the same

15. Giggly sounds

17. Note

18. Pontiac, e.g.

19. Xbox aficionados

20. Wired inn?

22. All in ___ work

23. Host of 'Paula's Home Cooking'

24. By way of, briefly

25. Patty Hearst's kidnap grp.

26. Asia's Trans ___ mountains

27. Looks good enough ___

28. Doctor, at times

31. "Act your ___!"

32. Ice cream parlor order

35. More rubicund

37. "I'll take that as ___"

38. St. Paul, for one

42. Arm parts

44. "My bad!"

45. "All Things Considered" airer

48. Longtime NFL coach Chuck

49. "I'm ___ you!"

50. Farm machine

52. Recharged one's batteries for a bit, as it were

54. Djibouti language

55. Break

56. From the beginning, in Latin

58. More authentic

59. Kind of shorts

60. Uses a knife

61. 'Taxi Driver' director

Down

1. Alpha's opposite

2. Wanderers

3. Sloth, e.g.

4. Cemetery, informally

5. Anatomical canals

6. Renoir's refusals

7. Mega Men retailer

8. Spectacles

9. '__ Like Alice'

10. Ninth Hebrew letter

11. Declaration from Dorothy

12. Nitwit

13. Waste

16. Toaster?

21. Dam

23. Hand (out)

26. Not many

27. Waste allowance

29. Beanery sign

30. Discordia's Greek counterpart

32. Amble

33. Springs

34. Widespread

36. Pattern of change or growth

39. College in New Rochelle, N.Y.

40. Fail

41. Mil. rank

43. Sodium, e.g.

46. Missouri feeder

47. Leans (on)

49. Humdingers

50. Boo-boo

51. ___ Janeiro

53. In __ (sulking)

54. Fodder holder

57. "Je te plumerai le __"

Puzzle #39
Life as a Vegetarian

Across

1. Fat Man and Little Boy, for two

7. Perturbed

15. State bordering Arizona

16. "Just because"

17. Chekov on "Star Trek"

18. Completely bare

19. Intertwine

20. 'Moonstruck' topic

21. Usher to a new spot

22. They're often taken by toddlers

23. A train?

26. Snoopy, e.g.

28. Bagel feature

29. Thing offered every time you go home even though you've been a vegetarian for years now

33. 'SNL"er for 13 seasons

35. __ vincit amor?

36. Subj. of a 1972 USA-USSR treaty

38. President in 1869

39. Spirit-lifter, perhaps

41. Generous giving

43. Disapproving sounds

44. Little angel

46. Naut. heading

47. Citi Field precursor

48. More like a Pepperland villain

53. Calls for attention

54. Got by

55. Certain cooking wines

58. Some video game consoles

59. Fancy salad vegetable

60. Washer setting

61. Baby's berth

62. Wipes out

Down

1. One posing

2. Kentucky folk hero

3. Law school newbies

4. Singer Janelle with 'Tightrope'

5. Yard sale items

6. Herbal quaff

7. Goodwill, e.g.

8. Standard

9. Yes, We ___

10. Forward thinkers

11. Storybook chapter

12. Enzyme suffix

13. NBA or NFL breaks

14. Navy rank (Abbr.)

23. Gauchos' gear

24. Fools

25. Al ___

27. Org. for operators?

28. Pacesetter

29. Newsgroup entries

30. Make ___ of

31. Eden figure

32. Canterbury cans

34. Kitchen gizmo

37. Spoil

40. Troop formation

42. Search through sale items

45. Old slang for a man's man

47. Lewis who voiced Hush Puppy

49. Turkish city known for its kebabs

50. Card game alternately known as 'pounce'

51. Ancient Roman magistrate

52. Four ___ (whiskey brand)

53. Coca-Cola founder Candler and politician Hutchinson

55. 2009 NYC Marathon winner Keflezighi

56. Simile center

57. Some colas

Puzzle #40
Number Goals

Across

1. Ticket numbers

7. Deodorant targets

14. Vivid red

15. 'Sorry, Charlie'

16. Tired toddler's demand

17. Set against

18. Treas. Isl. auth.

19. Has a hunch

21. 640 acres: Abbr.

22. Fed. agency created by the Civil Rights Act

24. Gets inedible

25. Come out on top

26. 'Nine' comb. form

28. Spot

30. Talk out of your head

31. Get comfy-cozy

33. Loverboy

35. Dude

37. Gaunt

40. Surrounded by

44. Larva, later

45. Qtys.

47. At hand, in poems

48. Artist Jean...

49. Campaign pros

51. Beaufort-scale category

52. Cambodian money

54. " __ fine lady upon ... "

56. Put in the Post, say

57. Cyber Monday beneficiary

59. Intellectual

61. Sicilian fortified wine

62. Obvious facts

63. Strengthen

64. They could double your dough

Down

1. Triangle type

2. Ministers

3. Blunder

4. Singer Joe and actor Ron

5. Mal -

6. Dictators' aides

7. Forebear

8. Down Under critters

9. CNN, the NYT, et al., in a somewhat pejorative internet acronym

10. There are 21 on a cube

11. Campaign about which Rumsfeld said in 2003 'it could last six days, six weeks - I doubt six

months'

12. End points

13. Predict, as the future

14. Hearth accessory

20. Sexy footwear

23. So on, in Latin

27. Zoologist's wings

29. Sicilian hot spot

30. __ to go

32. She, in Rome

34. Blood: Prefix

36. Transitory

37. 'Oh gawd...'

38. Bluenose

39. Looks

41. Most precious

42. Saudi salutations

43. In things

46. Not quite hailing

50. Physics Nobelist Emilio

53. Word after shopping or laundry

54. Vision starter

55. Río makeup

58. New Guinea port

60. Howdies

Across

1. Surfaces

8. "Om," e.g.

14. North Carolina's capital

15. Pillar of the Muslim community?

16. Figure

17. Consign

18. Toni Morrison's "___ Baby"

19. Adjusts

21. Prop up, or bite down

22. Some TV's

24. Muscle: Prefix

25. Intro to ene, or a Ukrainian river

26. "Night" author Wiesel

27. "La Bohème," e.g.

29. Congo river

30. Lover of Dido, in myth

32. Hardwood sources

34. Dump

36. Reserved

39. Be a go-between

43. Farm equipment

44. Kind of line

46. Old sketch-comedy show

47. "One of ___" (Willa Cather novel)

48. ___ Speedwagon

49. Arid

50. 'It ___ ...' (old-timey call from outside the door)

51. Riviera resort

55. Celtic Neptune

56. Extraction

58. Cache

60. Developed

61. Certifies

62. Remove the pits from

63. "Aha!"

Down

1. Asmara is its capital

2. Fetter

3. Transit vehicle through which the crime was "witnessed" in "12 Angry Men"

4. Riddle-me-___

5. Data entry acronym

6. Bavarian river

7. Forrest Gump's catch

8. In perfect condition

9. Aardvark fare

10. Veep under G.R.F.

11. Part of a board

12. Make over

13. Arrays

15. Hanukkah item

20. Jolt

23. Goes up and down

25. Outdo

27. "Hamlet" courtier

28. Kipling's wolf pack leader

31. Coolers, briefly

33. Clavell's "___-Pan"

35. Trimmed

36. Rotten

37. Hard to get

38. 1970's Ford Models

40. Neat

41. Fugue portions

42. High point

45. Attacks

51. Bank

52. Ancient

53. Illegal thing to cook

54. Numerical prefix

57. Spanish letter after "ka"

59. Abbr. after a name

ANSWERS

1

2

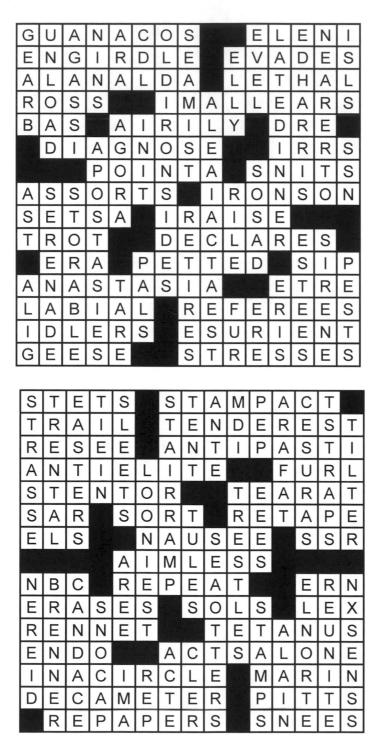

3

```
G U A N A C O S   █   E L E N I
E N G I R D L E   █   E V A D E S
A L A N A L D A   █   L E T H A L
R O S S   █   I M A L L E A R S
B A S   █   A I R I L Y   █   D R E █
█ D I A G N O S E   █   I R R S
    P O I N T A   █   S N I T S
A S S O R T S   █   I R O N S O N
S E T S A   I R A I S E
T R O T   D E C L A R E S
█ E R A   P E T T E D   █   S I P
A N A S T A S I A   █   E T R E
L A B I A L   R E F E R E E S
I D L E R S   E S U R I E N T
G E E S E   S T R E S S E S
```

4

```
S T E T S █ S T A M P A C T █
T R A I L █ T E N D E R E S T
R E S E E █ A N T I P A S T I
A N T I E L I T E █ F U R L
S T E N T O R █ T E A R A T
S A R █ S O R T █ R E T A P E
E L S █ N A U S E E █ S S R
    █ A I M L E S S █
N B C █ R E P E A T █ E R N
E R A S E S █ S O L S █ L E X
R E N N E T █ T E T A N U S
E N D O █ A C T S A L O N E
I N A C I R C L E █ M A R I N
D E C A M E T E R █ P I T T S
█ R E P A P E R S █ S N E E S
```

4

5

6

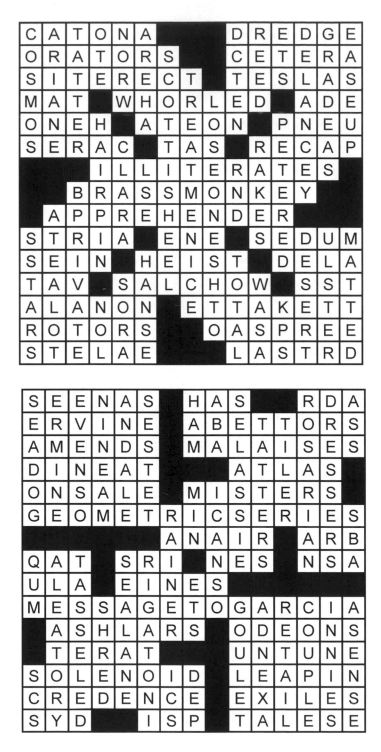

7

8

Puzzle 9

```
B L O S S O M ■ E T O I L E S
L A N T A N A ■ T A R B E L L
E N T E N T E C O R D I A L E
T E R N S ■ S L I P S ■ D E E
T O I T ■ A T I L T ■ H O S T
E N A ■ S C R E E ■ S O U S E
R E L A T I O N ■ B E L T E D
■ ■ R E D S T A R T S ■ ■ ■
I S L E T S ■ S C A T T E R S
S P A N S ■ S T A T S ■ A E S
S E S S ■ S H A D S ■ A R F S
U E A ■ B O I T E ■ A C N E S
E D G A R L E E M A S T E R S
R E N T I E R ■ E X C I S E S
S E A T E R S ■ S H I I T E S
```

9

Puzzle 10

```
A P P A R E L ■ S O N O R A N
M E E T E R S ■ E P O N I N E
S T A N D A T ■ M I R E D I N
T E S S A S ■ S E A E A G L E
E R A ■ S E C O ■ G L E E S
R A L E ■ S A U C E R S ■ ■
D R A W S ■ G N O M E ■ S N A
A N D R O M E D A S T R A I N
M O S ■ M A R L S ■ S A I N T
■ ■ T E A S E T S ■ S N E E
G E T U P ■ S S T S ■ T S A
R A I N L E S S ■ P A L L E T
U N S E A L S ■ D E N E U V E
M O H I C A N ■ O T A N K E R
P L A N E T S ■ D E A D E N S
```

10

11

12

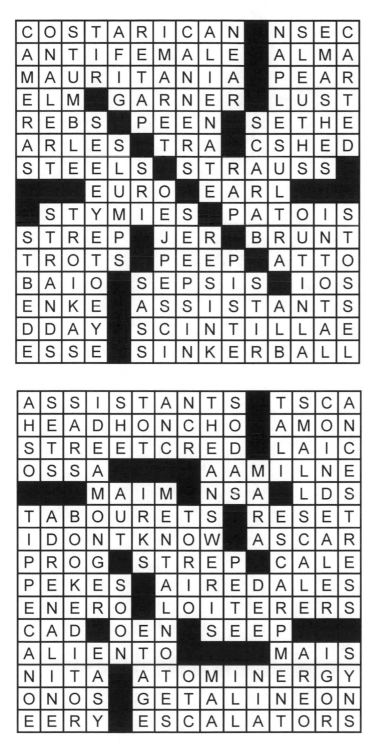

13

14

15

16

17

```
G R A N T O D . . . G A M A .
R E G A I N E D . A R C A N E
E V E N T I M E . P O U R I N
T I T . I C E C A P . P A L M
E L E A . E N R O L S . D I A
L E N D L . T E L E T H O N S
. . . R E T I E . P E O N E S
K E N O S H A . A I R B A S E
E L O I S E . T I E O N . . .
E A S T E R N E R . L O E W E
P S T . R U A N D A . B R E R
S T A S . L E A R N T . I C U
T I T T L E . N I G H T C A P
O C U L U S . T E E S H I R T
. S E E N . . S L E E V E S
```

18

```
R A M S E S I . B E R E A V E
E L A I N E S . A V O N L E A
F L I T T E R . T O O T E R S
R E N O S . A G T . T R A I T
I G L U . P E T E . H A S T O
E R I T . A L E N . A N T E D
S O N . T R I A S S I C . . .
. S E T U S . . C R E S T .
. . E R E C T E R S . E E S
U N M A N . A R N E . A A A S
N E A T S . R I T E . R E G S
S A U R O . C O R . S C A R S
A R M E N I A . A D P A G E S
F L E E T E R . P O O D L E S
E Y E S O R E . S A T E E N S
```

19

```
E P I C A R P   T H E S A M E
V A N P O O L   H O S T L E R
E N T E N T E C O R D I A L E
R A R A   L U A U S   S T A C
T C U     R E G     E N T
O H S O   P A S H A   O E I L
R E T A M E   A T T O R N E Y
    S U P E R S T A R
A S S E S S A S   I T I S S O
T E T S   I S A A C   S E E D
A V E     E L L     A M Y
C E R S   E M A I L   A M I S
O N E A R M E D B A N D I T S
S T O L E I N   I T S A L I E
T O S T A R T   S E C R E C Y
```

20

```
S P A D E C A S I N O   S T P
C E L E B R A T I O N   A R A
L O S E S O N E S T E M P E R
A N A S   C I R   I N A P E T
F I T     E S P O S I T O
F E I N   T R O A S   S E A N
  S A U C I E S T   S E R G E
  M O A S   I S A N
M E N E S   T A R T N E S S
O M A R   C O N E S   T E T O
N A N A N A N A   M U D
O N E T O N   P A D   L A D E
P A T E N T M E D I C I N E S
O T T   P O T S A N D P A N S
D E E   C O N T R A C O S T A
```

Grid 21:

```
A S N O . F I G . . . D R O P
S T O U T I S H . M O R E N O
P A S T R A M I . A P O D A L
C R E D I T S . S L I P S B Y
A E S O P . U A L N C Q U .
. E L D E S T . E A U D E
H O R S E O P E R A . P A G O
A V E . A M I L A T E . R E N
U E L E . I C E P E L L E T S
T R A S H . E S S E N E
. T Y C O O N S . O S S I E
C O R O N A E . P A R S O N S
O N A B E T . P O S T E R N S
D E C A Y S . G R E E N T E A
Y S E R . S T S . S A R I
```

21

Grid 22:

```
S T R I P E D . . C D L I
N E O L O G I C . S P R I N T
O N A L E A S H . T R U E T O
C D S . M L C A R R . G A R N
A T T N . S I N E A D . B A S
P O S E R . P E P P E R O N I
. S A D L Y . S N I V E L
B E A S T I E . V I O L E T S
I N L E T S . D E N T I
R A I S E C A I N . E N A C T
E M M . D O R S E Y . G R A E
M E E R . L A T E E N . A R S
E L N I N O . A R T E R I E S
S E T T E R . L E T M E S E E
. R S T U . D O O D E R S
```

22

23

```
A P E R I E S  ■ S H O T P A R
P A T I E N T  ■ T A V E R N A
T R A N S L I T E R A T I O N
N A L A ■ S C R A P ■ O M S K
E P I ■ ■ K A R ■ ■ E M E
S E A R ■ M Y N A S ■ F R I S
S T E E L Y ■ S T A R E S A T
■ S A L T P E T E R ■
P A N A T E L A ■ I S R A E L
I N O W ■ S A R E E ■ O S L O
C U T ■ ■ T E A ■ ■ A N O
A R A B ■ R U N T O ■ G R O K
R A T E S A R T E S T E A R S
O N E N A M E ■ R I O R I T A
S S S S S S ■ S E T T L E D
```

24

```
R E O S ■ S E E ■ ■ C S I S
A R R E S T E E ■ A T H E N E
S T A R T E R S ■ C A R E T S
T E N I E R S ■ E M P I R E S
A S T O R ■ C H E E S E S ■
■ U N S O R E ■ S T A T E
H O R S E O P E R A ■ O S A Y
O R E ■ R U I N E R S ■ O T E
B R A S ■ L A N A T U R N E R
S I C E M ■ T A L E S E ■
■ S H E A V E S ■ A S P C A
A R I S T O S ■ C O N T R O L
D O N A T I ■ M E U N I E R E
G O T W E T ■ A T T E N D E R
S T O S ■ L A S ■ G E R T
```

25

26

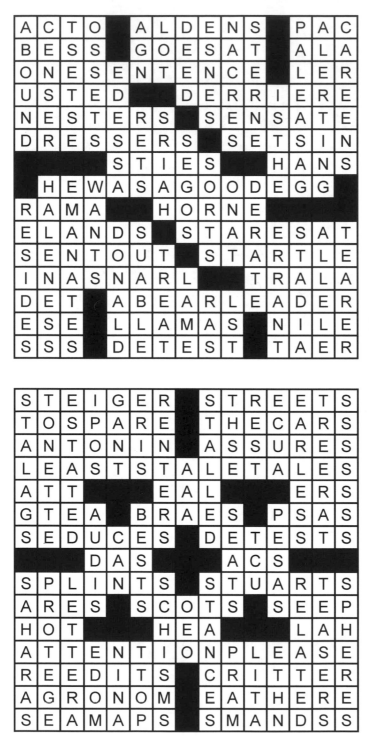

27

28

29

30

Puzzle 31

```
A S T H M A ■ ■ B O A S T E R
S W E E T S ■ A L A N H A L E
T I R A N A ■ T E T I A R O A
E N I D ■ S O T S ■ S T A H L
R E G S ■ E V I T A ■ T R I M
O F A ■ S T E R ■ L B E A M S
U L R I C ■ R E A L E R ■ ■ ■
T U R N R E D ■ L I T E R A L
■ ■ R O C O C O ■ A D E N O ■
R A T E D T ■ A H A S ■ A I D
E N O S ■ O T R A S ■ E S S E
E G R E T ■ H E S S ■ A S E S
D E R R I E R E ■ E M M E T T
E L E V A T O R ■ S I E S T A
D I S E A S E ■ ■ S A S S E R
```

31

Puzzle 32

```
P I V O T A L ■ ■ ■ S N I P S
A S I N I N E ■ O N E O C A T
R O S A N N A ■ R I V I E R A
A T O ■ S I S T I N E ■ B A R
D O R R ■ E E E E E ■ T E S T
E P E E S ■ S S N ■ K A R O L
R E D T A G ■ S T R A N G L E
■ ■ A T P R E S E N T ■ ■ ■
S N A K E O I L ■ A G A D I R
N O S E S ■ P A W ■ A R E T E
O T T S ■ G O T A T ■ A N E T
C E O ■ D E S E X E S ■ A M U
O P U L E N T ■ E N T E R I N
N A N E T T E ■ R E A L I Z E
E D D A S ■ ■ ■ S T Y M I E S
```

32

Puzzle 33

```
A T A G L A N C E ■ B E L G ■
M I N C E M E A T ■ A R E I N
U N O B L I G E D ■ N A I V E
L O U ■ Y E A S ■ E C O L E S
E R I E ■ S T A N D S F A S T
T E L L S ■ E R S E ■ N I L ■
S S H A P E D ■ A R C S I N E
■ ■ ■ N A M ■ L I U ■ ■
S H E D D E R ■ S E A P O R T
I O M ■ R A T E ■ O R F E O
C L A S S I F I E S ■ A C O T
K E I T E L ■ T H A T ■ A R R
A D L E R ■ S T E P A S I D E
S U M E R ■ A E R O K O R E A
■ P E N A ■ P R E R E C O R D
```

33

Puzzle 34

```
L A N A S ■ M I S S T A R T S
A P A R T ■ I R E N E C A R A
N I T T I ■ N A M E N A M E S
D A H ■ P A S T E L ■ I P S E
O S A ■ E S T E L L E ■ S S S
L A N I ■ C E L E S T A ■
E M I T ■ O R Y ■ T R A M P
G O E S A T ■ K E E N E R
S A L T S ■ D P I ■ C I N E
■ ■ O I L W E L L ■ A M A T
M A H ■ N E A T E N S ■ O T E
A D A S ■ G R E A S E ■ S A N
R E S T R A I N S ■ E M I R S
T E T E A T E T E ■ N O T M E
S P O N S O R E D ■ A B Y S S
```

34

Puzzle 35:

E	V	A	N	G	E	L	I	S	T	■	E	S	T	D
M	A	R	I	O	N	E	T	T	E	■	S	H	U	E
O	R	A	T	O	R	I	C	A	L	■	T	O	N	S
T	I	L	E	■	O	C	H	■	E	T	E	R	N	E
E	E	S	■	A	L	A	I	■	V	E	R	T	E	X
S	T	E	E	N	■	E	P	I	S	■	I	L	E	■
■	Y	A	X	E	S	■	R	E	S	T	L	E	S	S
■	■	I	M	O	N	■	S	E	T	I	■	■	■	■
A	N	A	T	O	L	I	A	■	D	U	C	A	T	■
B	I	D	■	N	O	E	S	■	■	B	E	N	E	T
S	C	H	L	E	P	■	A	R	S	E	■	Y	A	H
T	H	E	U	S	A	■	L	O	C	■	A	O	N	E
A	E	R	I	■	R	O	A	D	R	U	N	N	E	R
I	V	E	S	■	T	H	R	E	E	P	I	E	C	E
N	O	D	E	■	S	A	K	O	W	A	L	S	K	I

35

Puzzle 36:

C	A	C	H	E	T	■	S	U	B	T	L	E	■
A	T	A	S	T	E	■	E	A	R	H	A	R	T
M	E	R	E	C	A	S	H	S	W	E	A	T	E	R
P	A	L	■	H	O	M	E	S	■	A	T	A	L	E
A	T	O	P	■	R	I	S	I	N	■	A	K	O	N
R	O	A	L	D	■	T	S	O	R	O	■	I	N	T
I	N	D	O	O	R	■	O	N	O	N	D	A	G	A
■	■	N	Y	E	T	■	S	T	E	R	■	■	■
W	A	U	K	E	S	H	A	■	C	R	A	N	E	D
E	S	T	■	N	E	R	T	S	■	S	T	I	L	E
E	T	T	A	■	T	A	R	S	I	■	S	T	N	S
P	R	E	S	S	■	S	I	G	N	S	■	R	I	I
E	A	R	T	H	S	H	A	T	T	E	R	I	N	G
R	E	E	R	A	S	E	■	R	E	S	T	O	N	■
■	A	D	O	R	E	D	■	A	S	S	E	S	S	■

36

Grid 37:

```
O S C E O L A   A C A D E M E
P E R C H I K   A L G E R I A
A W E S O M E   M A S C O T S
L S A T   O G R E S   A D E E
S I T A     E S S A Y E R S
  M U T A T E S   I R S
U P R I S E S   M F A   T S R
E L E C T E E   A I R H O L E
Y E S   E T S   R E A I R E D
    S R O   R E S T A T E
A S S E N T E D     T I P S
W E L T   A D A P T   U L L A
F I E S O L E   H A S S L E S
U N E A T E N   D I S E A S E
L E T T E R S   S S S S S S
```

37

Grid 38:

```
O N A B I N G E   A T O M S
M O N O T O N Y   T E H E E S
E M I N E N C E   O T T A W A
G A M E R S   W W W H O T E L
A D A Y S   D E E N   T H R U
  S L A   A L A I   T O E A T
  R E F E R R E R   A G E
S U N D A E   R E D D E R
A N O   T W I N C I T Y
U L N A S   O O P S   N P R
N O L L   O N T O   B A L E R
T O O K A N A P   S O M A L I
E S C A P E   A B I N I T I O
R E A L E R   S E L E C T E D
  S L I T S   S C O R S E S E
```

38

39

40

41

Made in the USA
Middletown, DE
17 December 2016